THE STORY OF THE
MIAMI

CREATIVE   EDUCATION

Published by Creative Education
123 South Broad Street
Mankato, Minnesota 56001
Creative Education is an imprint of The Creative Company.

DESIGN AND PRODUCTION BY **EVANSDAY DESIGN**

PHOTOGRAPHS BY Associated Press, AP, Getty Images (Issac Baldizon
/ NBAE, Victor Baldizon / NBAE, Nathaniel S. Butler / NBAE, Tim
de Frisco / Allsport, Garrett Ellwood / NBAE, General Mills
for Business Wire, Otto Greule Jr. / Stringer, Vincent Laforet,
Daniel LeClaire / Newsmakers, D. Lippitt / Winstein / NBAE,
Andy Lyons / Allsport, Fernando Medina, Richard T. Nowitz /
National Geographic, Eliot J. Schechter / Allsport)

LIBRARY OF CONGRESS CATALOGING-IN-PUBLICATION DATA

Gilbert, Sara.
The story of the Miami Heat / by Sara Gilbert.
p. cm. — (The NBA—a history of hoops)
Includes index.
ISBN-13: 978-1-58341-413-2
1. Miami Heat (Basketball team)—History—
Juvenile literature. I. Title. II. Series.

GV885.52.M53G55 2006
796.323'64'09759381—dc22   2005051773

First edition

9 8 7 6 5 4 3 2 1

COVER PHOTO: *Dwyane Wade*

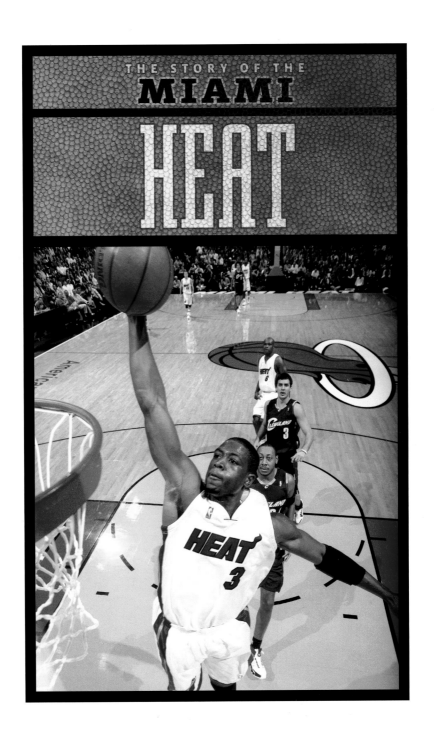

THE STORY OF THE
MIAMI
HEAT

SARA GILBERT

With his slicked hair,

TAILORED SUITS, AND SPIFFY SHOES, COACH PAT RILEY

LOOKED BETTER SUITED TO THE PAGES OF A FASHION

MAGAZINE THAN A BASKETBALL COURT. HIS ATTENTION

TO DETAIL WAS EVIDENT IN EVERYTHING FROM THE

KNOT OF HIS TIE, TO THE SHINE OF HIS SHOES...TO THE

EFFORT OF HIS TEAM. THE LONGTIME COACH WAS EVERY

INCH A CHAMPION, A HARD-DRIVING, QUICK-THINKING

WINNER WITH HIGH EXPECTATIONS OF HIMSELF AND

THOSE AROUND HIM. AND AFTER ARRIVING IN MIAMI

IN 1995, HE QUICKLY TURNED THE HEAT INTO A

FASHIONABLE CONTENDER AS WELL.

A COOL START

1

MIAMI, FLORIDA, IS KNOWN FOR ITS SUN, SAND, AND salsa beat. Located on the Florida peninsula's southeastern tip, Miami has a large Hispanic population that gives the city a Latin flavor that is clearly seen in its architecture, music, food, and many other aspects of local culture.

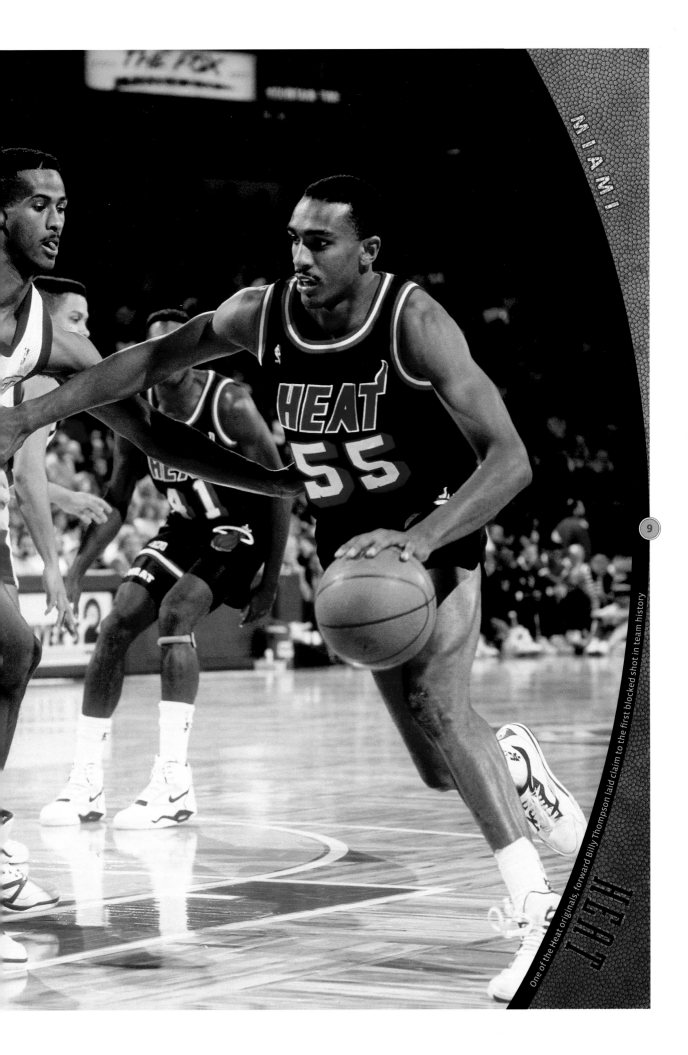

One of the Heat originals, forward Billy Thompson laid claim to the first blocked shot in team history

9

HEAT

Over six Miami seasons, Glen Rice averaged 19 points a game with his sweet outside shooting stroke

NBA

Florida is known as one of America's great sports states. It is home to numerous professional teams and some of college football's greatest rivalries. In 1988, the National Basketball Association (NBA) gave Miami's citizens a new professional team to support. In reference to the city's tropical climate, the basketball franchise was named the Miami Heat.

The first Heat roster was populated by veteran bench players such as forward Billy Thompson and guard Jon Sundvold. Fortunately, Miami chose well in its first NBA Draft, picking up forward Grant Long, shooting guard Kevin Edwards, and 7-foot center Rony Seikaly. These players learned many hard lessons as Miami went 15–67 in 1988–89.

Miami drafted well again in 1989, landing All-American forward Glen Rice and point guard Sherman Douglas. "The Heat have put together a nice group of kids," said Pat Riley, then the coach of the Los Angeles Lakers. "If they give them time to grow up, they'll have a good team." Still, the Heat remained cold, going just 18–64 and 24–58 the next two seasons.

BUFFETT GETS THE BOOT

Singer Jimmy Buffett, one of the Heat's biggest fans, is often seen sitting courtside at home games. But on February 4, 2001, the celebrity found himself in the spotlight, whistled for foul language. The Heat and the New York Knicks were playing in overtime (the Knicks won, 103–100) when Buffett was escorted to another seat in American Airlines Arena. "There was a little boy sitting next to him and a lady sitting by him," explained NBA referee Joe Forte. "He used some words he knows he shouldn't have used, so I asked security to move him to another location." The popular songwriter, known for such songs as "Cheeseburger in Paradise" and "Margaritaville," is still a regular Heat fan but has used his voice for singing, not heckling referees, since the incident.

ROLLING WITH RILEY

WITH THEIR TOP PICK IN THE 1991 NBA DRAFT, THE Heat selected guard Steve Smith, a 6-foot-8 former Michigan State University star equally skilled at passing, shooting, ball-handling, and rebounding. With his addition, the Heat began to improve. In 1991–92, the team went 38–44 and made the playoffs. But the powerful Chicago Bulls steamrolled Miami in three straight games.

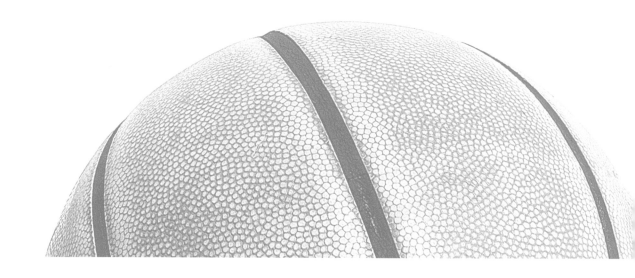

Versatile forward Steve Smith helped the Heat make the playoffs in two of his first three seasons in Miami

HEAT

14

Alonzo Mourning, who played two different stints for the Heat, took a combative approach to the game

After that first postseason appearance, hopes ran high in Miami. But Smith and key reserve forward Willie Burton missed much of the 1992–93 season with injuries, and the Heat fell short in the playoff race. "We're not kids anymore," proclaimed Rice before the start of the next season. "The fans have been patient with us. Now it's time to reward them."

The Heat posted their best record yet in 1993–94, going 42–40, but they were knocked out in the first round of the playoffs by the Atlanta Hawks. Then, during the off-season and into the 1994–95 campaign, the entire organization underwent a drastic upheaval. Seikaly, Smith, and Long were traded away; forwards Billy Owens and Kevin Willis were brought in; and coach Kevin Loughery was replaced by Alvin Gentry. But when the Heat finished 32–50, well out of playoff contention, Gentry too was fired.

In 1995, Miami finally found the leader it needed: Pat Riley, who came on board as both the team's president and head coach. Riley had won three NBA championships during his 13-year coaching career with the Lakers and the New York Knicks, and his teams had never failed to make the

BATTLE AT MADISON SQUARE GARDEN

Emotions ran high as the Heat squared off against the rival New York Knicks in Game 4 of the first round of the 1998 playoffs, and Alonzo Mourning got into a punching match with his one-time teammate, Larry Johnson. But tension turned to comedy when diminutive Knicks coach Jeff Van Gundy wrapped himself around Mourning's leg, closed his eyes, and held on for dear life in an effort to break up the fight. Both Mourning and Johnson were suspended for fighting, but Van Gundy's only punishment was seeing his picture in the newspapers the next day. "I looked like a fool," he admitted. "I wasn't going through a normal thought process at that very moment." It wasn't so funny for the Heat, however, when the Knicks won Game 5 and the series.

playoffs. "We're going to build this franchise into a winner the only way I know how," he said. "We're going to bring in the best players, and we'll work harder than anybody else."

Riley's first step was to acquire a great center. On the night before the 1995–96 season opener, he traded Rice and two other players to the Charlotte Hornets for All-Star center Alonzo Mourning. The 6-foot-10 and 260-pound Mourning was one of the most intimidating players in the league. Because of his great defensive ability, Mourning's offensive skills had often been overlooked. But in Miami, he blossomed into a 20-plus points-per-game scorer and a top rebounder.

Riley also put together a trade with the Golden State Warriors for All-Star guard Tim Hardaway, another fierce competitor. By the end of the 1995–96 season, the Heat had virtually a new roster and were back in the playoffs. Although Miami was swept by the Chicago Bulls, the tone was set. Miami's days as a league doormat were over.

MIAMI

17

HEAT

Tim Hardaway was famous for his quick drives to the basket and almost unstoppable "crossover" dribble

TRYING FOR A TITLE

IN 1996–97, THE HEAT'S REMODELED ROSTER STORMED to a 61–21 record. Mourning was among the NBA's leaders in scoring, rebounding, and blocked shots, while Hardaway poured in 20 points and dished out nearly 9 assists a game. Guards Voshon Lenard and Dan Majerle added deadly three-point shooting and hard-nosed defense, while power forward P.J. Brown gave Miami an enforcer on the boards.

Long-range marksman Voshon Lenard made headlines with eight three-pointers in one game in 1997

Whether fighting for loose balls or boxing out for rebounds, P.J. Brown gave his all for Miami

In the postseason, the Heat finally won their first playoff series, defeating the Orlando Magic in five games. Then, after falling behind the New York Knicks—whom Riley had coached from 1991 to 1995—in a second-round series, Miami rallied to win three straight games and advance to the Eastern Conference Finals. The Heat were just one series away from the NBA Finals, but the Chicago Bulls—on their way to a fifth title in seven years—then ended Miami's season.

Even as Mourning sat out with a knee injury for part of 1997–98, Miami rolled to a 55-27 record. In the playoffs, the Heat again faced New York. The teams split the first four games, but an altercation late in Game 4 proved devastating for the Heat. Mourning and Knicks forward Larry Johnson (former teammates with the Charlotte Hornets) got tangled up under the basket and exchanged punches. Both were ejected and suspended for Game 5. Without their star center, the Heat lost 98-81.

The next two seasons were bitter replays of the same story: The Heat won big during the regular season but were knocked out of the postseason by the rival Knicks. After their third straight playoff loss to New York in 2000, the Heat shuffled their lineup by sending Brown and forwards Jamal

MOURNING'S SICKNESS Just before the 2000–01 season began, Alonzo Mourning was diagnosed with focal glomerulosclerosis, a kidney disease that destroys the tiny filters that remove waste from the blood. "Right now, my main objective is to get healthy," he said, "so I live my life normally, so I can can see my babies grow up, so I can enjoy my family and possibly do the thing that I know and love—the game of basketball." Determined to keep the chronic ailment at bay, Mourning began taking as many as 14 pills a day and played sparingly over the next four seasons. After a kidney transplant in 2003, he returned to the Heat (after playing briefly for the New Jersey Nets) in time to boost the team's 2005 playoff run, playing valuable minutes as a backup to center Shaquille O'Neal.

Mashburn and Otis Thorpe to the Charlotte Hornets for guard Eddie Jones and forward Anthony Mason. The Heat added more inside muscle by signing 6-foot-9 forward Brian Grant.

Unfortunately, Miami was dealt a terrible blow when Mourning was diagnosed with a serious kidney ailment that sidelined the All-Star for most of the 2000–01 season. Still, the team vowed to carry on the fight. "Alonzo is our leader, but this is an opportunity for the rest of us to lead in his absence," said Dan Majerle. "We won't quit, because we owe that to 'Zo."

The short-handed Heat fought their way to a 50–32 record and the playoffs, but they were then swept by the Hornets in three straight games. Mourning returned the next season, but Hardaway was now gone. The Heat's chemistry seemed to go cold, and Miami missed the playoffs for the first time in seven years with a disappointing 36–46 record.

HEAT

Known for his dreadlocked hair and relentless hustle, Brian Grant spent four seasons in a Heat uniform

HUSTLE STATS

MIAMI
DETROIT

REB 19 OFF 3 DEF 17 STLS 4
17 6 11 2

27 6:16 QTR 2 36 DET 1 TUL
1 5

HEAT

Often the speediest player on the court, guard Eddie Jones excelled at running and finishing fast breaks

CHAMPIONSHIP HEAT

4

THE 2001–02 SEASON MARKED THE FIRST TIME THAT

Pat Riley's team failed to make the playoffs. Mourning

was sidelined for most of the next season, and although

Jones and young forward Caron Butler treated fans to

solid efforts, Miami went just 25–57 and missed the

postseason again. At the end of that season, Riley an-

nounced that he was leaving the bench to concentrate

solely on being team president.

Things didn't start well for Miami's new head coach,

Stan Van Gundy, as the 2003–04 Heat lost their first

seven games. But as the season progressed, so did the

play of high-flying rookie guard Dwyane Wade and vet-

eran forward Lamar Odom. By the season's end, the

Heat had assembled a 42–40 record, good enough to re-

turn to the playoffs. The Heat topped the New Orleans

Hornets in round one but then fell to the Indiana Pacers.

27

Athletic forward Caron Butler turned heads as just a rookie in 2002–03, averaging 15 points a night

Shaquille O'Neal starred for both of Florida's NBA teams, having spent four seasons with the Orlando Magic

Before the 2004–05 season, Miami made a blockbuster trade with the Los Angeles Lakers, acquiring superstar center Shaquille O'Neal for three players. "Today the Miami Heat took a giant step forward in our continued pursuit of an NBA championship for the city of Miami and this franchise," said Riley. With O'Neal on board, the Heat returned to the playoffs and won two series to earn the right to battle the defending NBA champion Detroit Pistons in the 2005 Eastern Conference Finals. Injuries hobbled the Heat, though, and Miami lost the series in seven dramatic games.

Encouraged by the near-miss, the Heat then made more dramatic roster moves, loading up with veterans such as forward Antoine Walker and point guards Jason Williams and Gary Payton. It took some time for the new lineup to jell, but after Riley returned as head coach in midseason and installed a tougher brand of defense, Miami rolled to a 52–30 mark and the division championship. The Heat swiftly turned that into a conference championship, as they won two playoff series and then knocked off the Pistons to reach the NBA Finals.

BREAKFAST OF SHAQ   Odds are that Shaquille O'Neal had a big bowl of Wheaties cereal for breakfast on any given day, probably from a box with his picture on it. In March 2005, he joined the ranks of such NBA greats as George Mikan, Kareem Abdul-Jabbar, and Wilt Chamberlain when General Mills unveiled a box of Wheaties with his picture on it. "O'Neal has distinguished himself as the most celebrated player in basketball today," said Eric Treschuk, marketing manager for Wheaties. "We are thrilled to add him to the list of renowned athletes who have graced the cover of the Wheaties package through the years." Shaq was humbled by the announcement. "I grew up idolizing the great athletes who were on the Wheaties box," he said. "That's why it's such an honor for me to become part of the Wheaties family."

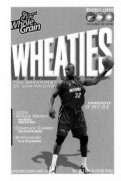

Energized Miami fans were left suddenly glum as their team was thrashed by the Dallas Mavericks in Games 1 and 2 of the Finals and fell behind by 13 points with just 7 minutes to play in Game 3. But the Heat then found their swagger again. Led by the smart play of their veterans and the clutch scoring of Wade—who cemented his status as an NBA superstar by averaging 34 points a game during the Finals—the Heat stormed back to win Game 3, then swept the next three contests as well to bring home the title and spark a giant party in Miami. "The great Pat Riley told me we were going to win today," O'Neal said after the series-clinching Game 6. "I didn't have the best game. But D-Wade's been doing it all year. He's the best player ever."

In their short history, the Miami Heat have relied on hard work and a never-say-die attitude to rise from modest expansion roots and become the league's best team. After finally celebrating their first NBA championship, Florida's sports-crazy fans are already eager for another championship Heat wave to roll over the city of Miami.

BEAUTIFUL BALL PLAYER

Dwyane Wade couldn't wait to distribute copies of *People* magazine to all of his teammates on April 29, 2005. That's because Miami's star guard—best known for his explosive quickness and acrobatic shot-making—had been listed among the magazine's "50 Most Beautiful People" in the issue that came out that day. "All of them will get a copy, no question," Wade said. "I might hand-deliver it to their rooms." Wade, one of four athletes on the list and the only NBA star included, was delighted to be mentioned in the magazine. His teammates, however, were dreading the inevitable boasting. "We're going to be hearing about this for the rest of the year," guard Damon Jones said. Shortly after appearing on the list, Wade was also chosen to serve as ambassador for the fashionable Sean John clothing line.

HEAT

Jason Williams's flashy passing and 12-points-per-game scoring average helped make the Heat NBA champs

31